# THE LAST MOVE OF GOD

EMMANUEL OLUFEMI AYEKOLOYE

**The Last Move of God**

Published by Seed Publishing House

# DEDICATION

To God the Father, Son and Holy Spirit.

# Preface

WHILE thinking about the Russia-Ukraine war, Jesus revealed to me a profound revelation about the unfolding End-Time events marking the ultimate end of the world. This revelation is divine and not an assumption. A divine revelation shows that an unstoppable spiritual revival will spread like a sweeping volcano in the coming days. The entire world will see the true Messiah, Jesus, when he appears in the sky to save mankind.

The Holy Spirit is my navigator as I use the words of God to lead believers of the second coming of Christ into the ship of eternal life.

My goal has been to abolish the embargo of ignorance, closed-mindedness, emptiness, and uncertainty about the end times, and prepare their minds for the approaching arrival of Christ. My prayer is that you receive your liberty from the grip of Satan and uphold the truth which is by Jesus Christ. I recommend you to read this literal eschatology book. Read it, understand it, consume it, imbibe it, and reflect on it constantly. It will be my joy if at the end of time we all meet at the city of God, amen.

# THE LAST MOVE OF GOD

# CONTENTS

# CHAPTER ONE
## THE LAST MOVE OF GOD

THE WORLD is approaching the second coming of Jesus Christ, leading to the end of the world. Christ's arrival is drawing near and only those who have the wisdom to understand times and seasons like the wise men from the east at Jesus' birth can comprehend this. Jesus Christ's second coming will occur in different ways. It will range from a grand display of God's power to a sudden demonstration of God's restorative work for all believers in Christ. The coming of Christ will manifest as Parousia, Apocalypsis, and Epiphaneia.

## PAROUSIA

Matthew 24:3

And as he sat upon the mount of Olives, the disciples came unto him privately, saying, "tell us, when shall these things occur?" And what shall be the sign of thy coming, and of the end of the world?

First Thessalonians 4:15-17

According to Jesus own words which state that those who are alive will not rapture before those who had died, the Lord will come down (Parousia) from heaven with a loud shout, the voice of the archangel with the trumpet call of God and the dead in Christ will rise first; followed by those that are alive and shall remain with him forever.

The Parousia brings the rapture and the resurrection of the dead.

## APOCALYPSIS

You do not lack any spiritual gift as you eagerly await the Revelation (Apocalypsis) of our Lord Jesus Christ. He will strengthen you till the end so that you are faultless on the day of our Lord Jesus Christ.

I encourage Christians to stay strong while awaiting the revelation of Christ. The revelation of Christ brings judgement upon unbelievers and brings blessings and glory to Christians.

## EPIPHANEIA

Titus 2:11-13

The revelation of God's grace, which brings salvation, has been made known to all.

It teaches us to reject ungodliness and worldly desires and to live self-controlled, righteous, and devout lives in this present time, while we anxiously await the blessed hope and glorious appearance (Epiphaneia) of our magnificent God and Savior, Jesus Christ. The return of Christ is a source of hope for Christians. The Parousia, Apocalypsis, and

Epiphaneia all describe either one event or multiple events occurring simultaneously when scrutinized.

# CHAPTER TWO
## THE COMING OF CHRIST

IN ORDER to comprehend Christ's last move, we must first understand why he came in the beginning. What requires the need for his second coming, considering what he established and accomplished? The first coming of Christ was inevitable by the fall of Adam in the garden of Eden.

### Adam and Eve
God made Adam a king and the crown of his creation and made Eve his companion and put them in

the garden of Eden. He gave them authority and dominion over all his creations. In Eden, God used to fellowship with them in the evenings, as it was a place of rest, comfort, and abundance.

In heaven, Satan planned a coup and then God banished him to earth, where Adam had jurisdiction over him. Satan infiltrated the garden of Eden and became a tempter to Adam and Eve. The deception of Satan led Adam and Eve to disobey God and incurred His wrath. Satan took away their authority and dominion, resulting in them becoming slaves to Satan and sin.

God's instant judgement fell upon the three offenders,

beginning with Satan, the Devil.

Genesis 3:14-15
God said to the serpent, "Because you have done this, I cursed you above all cattle and every beast of the field. You will crawl on your belly and eat dust for the rest of your life, as I create hostility between you and the woman, and between your offspring and hers. He will strike your head and you will strike his heel."

Chased from the garden, Satan crawled on his belly.
God turned to Adam and rained curses on the ground.

In Genesis 3:17-19,
Since you listened to your wife

and ate from the forbidden tree, against my command. By the sweat of your brow, you shall eat bread until you return to the earth, for I made you of dust and will return to dust.

The ground did not offend God, so Satan saw it as God's partiality in judgement and had since been wagging war against God's creations, particularly man.

God said to Eve, I will very much increase your pain in childbearing. Giving birth will be a sorrowful experience, and you will have a deep longing for your husband, who will be your ruler.

Since the fall of Adam, man has an inborn sinfulness which

affected every part of his human personality-body, soul and spirit and had culminated into original sin and had remained a mystery. By this sin, Adam rejected God and became master of his own life. We, also as descendants of Adam, have rebelled against God so that all men became sinners. The characteristics feature of sin is that it is against God. By this singular action of Adam, sin has removed us far away from God and we are constantly under his wrath and man became God's enemy.

Since then, humanity has been in a desperate condition without Christ, unable to save ourselves from sin and death, relying entirely on God for deliverance. The ungodliness and unrighteousness of men made them to be holding the truth of God in unrighteousness. Despite all this, God still loves us and has provided a perfect way of escape. His love and mercy moved him to offer his only son for our pardon.

John 3:16

"For God so loved the world, that he gave his only begotten son, that whosoever believes in him should not perish but have everlasting life"

God sent his son into the world for salvation, not condemnation, and those who have faith in him are not subject to condemnation, but those who do not believe in the name of God's only begotten son are already condemned.

At his first coming, God gave Jesus three assignments for the salvation of mankind:
(I) Justification
(II) Sanctification and
(III) Glorification

Jesus fulfilled two assignments: justification and sanctification, and assured his return for the glorification of the saints, having experienced glorification Himself.

John 14:1-3

Keep your heart free from trouble; if you have faith in God, have faith in me too. There are multiple mansions in my father's house. If it weren't true, I would have let you know. I go to prepare a place for you. Once I've made a place ready for you, I'll come back to get you and bring you to where I am. Wherever I am, you can also be there.

To make his work easier on salvation and sanctification, Jesus laid the foundation of the church like a refiner fire and a purifier oven.

# CHAPTER THREE
## PURPOSE OF HIS COMING

THE ATONEMENT (AT-ONE-MENT) Once and for all. This is the means by which God dealt with sin in order to bring man into fellowship with himself. The death of Christ dealt with the problem of sin and has brought believers into fellowship with God. The Levitical sacrifice of old pointed forward to the death of Jesus Christ as the grounds of the forgiveness of God.

Leviticus 17:11

The blood brings about a reconciliation for one's life.

Hebrews 9:22
Forgiveness of sin is only possible through the shedding of blood. The blood of Jesus is what eradicated all curses on human beings, fertility, and the land.

The cross is the basis of our relationship with God. By bearing the burden of human sins, Christ's crucifixion enabled God, who is holy, to accept sinful humans. Christ's blood is the atonement for cleansing from sin and a removal of guilt. Christ's death justifies sinners through grace, unmerited favor, and God's acceptance.

Through conversion, you have changed from God's enemy to becoming his friend, and have reconciled with him. The previously lifeless spirit is now revitalized and awakened, capable of perceiving God's messages through intuition. It restored the communication channel between God and the soul, enabling effective communion.

The conscience, once scorched, now yearns for righteousness. The soul and the body can now relate to and submit to the spirit. All the evil reports concerning you in the record book of God are now wiped clean by the blood of Jesus. The blood of Jesus will also cleanse you from sin, eradicate sin in your life, erase the handwritten laws that were against you, and remove curses and enchantments that are contrary to you nailing them on the cross. However, you are not completely clean. As you remain faithful, the Holy Spirit will anchor and strengthen your faith, keeping you steadfast in the Gospel. You will have redemption through his blood, and this is the root of your salvation. Jesus knows you'll still sin, but the Holy Spirit will warn you of planned sin and convict you of actual actions.

You will experience continual refreshment and sanctification as the Holy Spirit works in you through genuine repentance. God's love is universal hence, he wants everyone to be saved and has made salvation for the saints accessible through Jesus' sacrifice on the cross. Christ's death is sufficient for all, but only those who believe in him will reap the benefits, not everyone. The cross has the power to draw all men to Christ, but the sinful man cannot accept Christ because his will is in bondage to his sinful nature. But Christ's death has purchased powerful incentives which break down man's sinful resistance to Christ, which enables everyone that is free to choose and accept or reject Christ.

The Bible is clear that not all will accept God's free salvation offer. There are those who will secure their own salvation through prophets or deities, leading to eternal damnation. Many people will accept salvation through Christ, leading to eternal life.

Revelation 5:9

And they sang a new song, saying: "You are worthy to take the scroll and to open its seals, because you were slain, and with your blood you purchased for God persons from every tribe and language and people of nations"

Jesus used his blood to purchase salvation for the saints.

Revelation 7:9-10

Following this, I witnessed an immense multitude, beyond counting, people from every nation, tribe, ethnicity, and language. They were standing in front of the throne and the Lamb, adorned in white robes and holding palm branches. And they cried with a loud voice saying "Salvation to our God, who sits upon the throne and unto the lamb."

## CHRIST AND THE CHURCH

Christ came to save the world and not to change the world. He came with the gospel of God and not politics. Gospel and politics are poles apart, but those who play politics can embrace the gospel of Christ, receive salvation and gain eternal life. Jesus revealed the vision of the church to his apostles at Caesarea Philippi.

Matthew 16:18

"I will build my church and the gate of hell shall not prevail against it."

The Apostles received the responsibility of achieving its fulfillment.

When Christ was rounding up his own assignment, he commissioned his disciples to effect what he came to establish; the church.

Matthew 28:19
"Go therefore and make disciples of all nations baptizing them in the name of the Father and of the Son and of the Holy Spirit teaching them to observe all things that I have commanded you, and lo, I am with you always even to the end of the world."

A disciple is a learner, an imitator of his teacher, he acts and live like him. He is an adherent who sticks and holds fast to the word and doctrine of his leader. Jesus told them to go into the world and conform men and women to his image and make them like himself through the instrumentality of his word and commandments given to them. The Apostles laid the pattern for the work of conformity and handed over the baton to the New Testament Ministers; men and women chosen divinely to carry on the work.

Ephesians 4:11

Jesus appointed certain individuals as apostles, prophets, evangelists, pastors, and teachers to prepare the saints for their ministry tasks. With the purpose of building up the community of believers, until we all reach a common faith and understanding of the son of God, striving towards spiritual maturity and becoming fully like Christ.

Jesus Christ first selected these men and women as his own and then granted them as valuable assets to the church - the assembly of those who have been delivered from the detrimental influence and repercussions of sin. They are now ready to be transformed into the likeness of their senior brother and Lord Jesus Christ. The underlying motive is to disciple people after Jesus when they themselves have become like Jesus.

The purpose of God from the beginning, in wanting Adam and Eve and their offspring to possess the earth in righteousness, holiness, and purity, has not changed. However, Satan and Adam annulled it, but it is now being reinforced and nearing completion in Christ Jesus. Jesus promised his followers that he will come back for them to complete his assignment on Glorification.

John 14:2-3
My father's house contains many mansions. If it were not so, I would have told you. I go to prepare a place for you. I'll go and prepare everything for you, and then I'll bring you along.

Christ's return may manifest as

a gradual wave, likened to a two-edged sword, piercing and dividing the soul and spirit, demonstrating God's power for the restoration of true believers in the church.

Matthew 24:36

But of that day and hour no man knows, not even the Angels of heaven but my Father only. In a field, two individuals will be present, but only one will remain while the other departs. At the mill, two women will be grinding; one will be taken, and the other left. Be ready, for the Lord will come at an hour you least expect.

All indices concerning the church and the world show that the last move of our Lord Jesus Christ is imminent. Therefore, let us not sleep as others do, but let us watch and be sober. The time is imminent, so let us put a stop to all fleshly distractions that characterized our frivolous religious ceremonies. The church activities are no more spiritual and the church is no more spirit-filled. Christ abhors all the worthless celebrations that have plagued the shameless jubilation. These things can deafen our ears to the sound of his approaching. We should not allow our hearts to be weighed down with deceitfulness of riches, as many have turned the church to business center. Enjoyment of life, drunkenness and cares of life by saints may stiffen and deafen their souls to this coming visitation by Christ. There is ample evidence encouraging us to start watching all around us. The backsliding state of the church is enough to spur us to gird our loins, but many of us cannot see by ourselves the correct position we are because of the delusion that is resting upon us and the church. Because of this, our vision could not expose our worthlessness, iniquity and guilt hence, our true condition remains hidden from us. That is why everyone is right to justify every surfaced condition in his or her life differently from the version of what God says. If Jesus were to arrive at this moment, a lot of us would be ineligible for the rapture because of the heavy burden of unacknowledged defilement we carry.

Observing the development of science in the world today, the development of nuclear armament, production of life destructive machines and plants, satellite communication network, regional unification, single currency rationalization, and one-world-order projects are strategies towards liquidation of the world.

With the proliferation of nuclear arsenal and the desire to maintain power supremacy by world leaders shows that the life-span of the world now looks fragile. God will wait for the New Testament leaders and ministers to prepare the church of Christ before moving forward in fulfilling the world prophesies for Jesus to come. It does not really matter what teachers, pastors and Prophets declare from the pulpits, irrespective of those inspiring and motivational messages, the heavens know those who are in constant touch with it and heaven knows that as the church is today is unprepared for the coming of Jesus Christ. Many things are wrong that the church must put right. God is calling and revealing himself to fresh men of God who could convict the heart of believers and unbelievers to spirituality instead of the present rat-race for wealth and the building of earthly empires.

# CHAPTER FOUR
## CHRIST SPIRITUAL VISITATION

AT CHRIST'S second coming, he will surely fulfill the outstanding fulfillment of Glorification, while the last times events are already unfolding. The heightened awareness of the present time is a wake up call.

Romans 13:11-14
It's time to wake up from sleep because our salvation is closer than when we first believed. The night is far spent; the day is at hand; let us therefore cast off the works of

darkness and let us put on the armor of light. Let us walk honestly as in the day, not in strife and envying, but put ye on the Lord Jesus and make no provision for the flesh, to fulfill the lust thereof.

We need no seer to convince us of the darkness that has enveloped the earth and the church. War, suffering, and uncertainty are spreading across the entire world. It is just a matter of time before deep darkness overshadows everything. It is important to note that the church needs the Lord to arise for cleansing and purification in order for us to see the glory of the Lord upon us. The coming of the Lord is the arising of the Lord upon the church in the power of his word like a refiner's fire.

Malachi 3:2-3

"But who can stand when he appears? For he is like a refiner's fire and a Fuller's soap. He will sit as a refiner and a purifier of silver. He will purify the sons of Levi and purge them as gold and silver so that they may offer to the Lord an offering of righteousness."

Those who are consumed by envy, pride, covetousness, bitterness, and selfishness will experience the development of monkey pox in their bodies. There will be cold sweat on their forehead because they want to resurrect without dying.

God's glory will not come until fire has consumed all the vices in them. The sharp two-edge sword of Christ must separate us from all evil and corrupt attachments of sin and self in our lives.

Those who can endure and desire genuine separation will experience purification and the purging process, which will unveil the glory of our Lord Jesus Christ upon them.

Malachi 4:1-3

The Lord says that a day is coming when fire will consume the proud and wicked, leaving nothing behind. For those who fear my name, the sun of righteousness will bring healing and prosperity. They will go forth and thrive, like well-nourished calves, and they will triumph over the wicked. On the day I do this, they shall be like ashes under the sole of your feet, says the Lord of hosts.

The importance of watching cannot be over-emphasized.

Jesus says in Luke 21:36,
Watch therefore and pray always that you may be counted worthy to escape all these things that will come to pass, and stand before the son of man.

What does watching in such a time as this entails? First is the ability to discern. We need to recognize and comprehend the signs that point out God's forthcoming actions, so we can collaborate with him when the time comes. If you cannot discern the symptoms of a sickness, you will have less concern for clinical check up. Without discernment, the world's problems, Christianity's state, and your own lifestyle may go unnoticed. Without seeing things for what they truly are, you won't feel motivated to take action. To be without discerning is to be like the hypocritical Pharisees of Jesus' days who, though, could discern the face of the sky but could not discern the signs of their time, and they missed God's best for their generation.

Second is the State of preparedness. We must be ready to listen and follow Christ's guidance as he addresses areas that need improvement in our lives and ministries. If we predetermine what and how to hear, holding on to our own preconceived notions, doctrines and irrational preferences, we sure shall become blind to the things God has designed for our peace and restoration.

The Pharisees leading the jews in Jesus' time were authority in matters of the law, yet they failed to locate the words of Jesus in their scriptures because they closed their eyes and God decreed concerning them.

Matthew 13:14-15
"Hearing you will hear and shall not understand, and seeing you will see and not perceive, for the heart of these people has gone dull, their ears are hard of hearing and their eyes they have closed, lest they should see with their eyes

and hear with their ears and turn, so that I should heal them."

It is quite easy to be so busy defending what God said in the past that we trample under feet what he is saying in the present. The Pharisees' problem was that they did not realize they were defending a law caked with the dust of prejudice, self-interest, and human tradition. A touch of God's breath is all the law needed to be gloriously reborn. It is for this purpose that Jesus appeared in their midst to make the law a living thing in their hearts, but they rejected him because they determined to have nothing to do with him and it became their corruption.

Prophet Micah says of them.

Micah 7:4
"The best of them is a brier, the most upright is sharper than a thorn-hedge. The day of thy watchmen and thy visitation has come, now shall be thy perplexity."

The Equipping of the saints:
John 4:23
"But the hour is coming and now is when the true worshippers will worship the Father in spirit and in truth: for the father is seeking such to worship him."

This burden is on seeking a private encounter and building a consistent communion with the Lord.

Christ is tired of our spiritual vagueness with the crowds and multitude in the Churches and the public worship amid all religious fanfares of our present day. When heaven wants to help a man. It gives him secret keys to greatness. The Lord Jesus, despite that he was too busy ministering in public, often withdraw privately to spend ample time with the Father.

Matthew 14:23

"And when he had sent the multitude away, he went up into a mountain apart to pray: and when the evening was come, he was there alone."

Many things are wrong in the church that needs to be put right, standard shifted must be restored, misplaced priorities must be re-ordered, all the realities that have been replaced with shadows and frivolities must be reinstated, many things which have been unequally yoked with the ideals of church life must be separated and cast out otherwise Satan the enemy of God will open his mouth wide against the Lord Jesus Christ and his church hoping to gnash his teeth and say, "I have swallowed the church," but God forbid.

Whether you are a young Convert, Apostle, Pastor, Prophet, Evangelist, Teacher, Bishop, Deacon, Deaconess or Elder, the sole purpose of your calling is that you should commune adequately with the Lord privately.

Private encounters are crucial

as the world faces an impending tribulation, where public gatherings may become impossible, much like during the COVID-19 pandemic.

Matthew 24:6-7a
Wars and rumors of wars are expected, so don't let them trouble you.

Nation will rise against nation and kingdom against kingdom as this prophecy of Jesus Christ is an open manifestation in our public space. War drums sound in every corner of the world today, where conflict persists. Nations are stockpiling weapons and building war armament, disregarding humanity's welfare.

Moving further, the church has a greater role to play now than ever before. Believers should possess a sound foundation in the word of God and fortified faith to conquer the impending danger facing the world and the church. Christian leaders should brace up effectively and play their salvation role in saving the saints on the face of these perverse nations whose joy and pride is on the number of innocent people killed and the amount of blood they shed and spilled unnecessarily without showing remorse for their crime. The church itself will experience severe persecution by authorities in government. Many present-day Christians face challenges with unfulfilled desires for God's presence owing to a lack of knowledge and support from leaders. They have spent many of their days in confusion and regret because they are not always in God's presence. Amidst this prevailing spiritual apathy, the church should educate its members to seek more than a superficial spiritual encounter.

"Whom do I have in heaven but you? And on earth, there is nothing else that I desire," David affirmed in Psalm 73:25.

Their lives must be a torrent of perpetual spiritual desire. As we progressively have regular encounters with the Lord. privately, the Holy Spirit will move through the tides and stimulate us towards constant fellowship with the Lord. Prophetic words from ministers of God may come into your life, but they alone cannot take you to heaven. No matter how many deliverance sessions you undergo with anointing, you will yet be far away from realizing your spiritual desire. Divine power to achieve your heart's desires can only be achieved by desiring to dwell in his presence.

A lot of Christians are sweating at old age because of disappointments, failures and struggles when they should be resting.

David boldly declared in Psalm 16:8-9 "I have set the Lord always before me because he is at my right hand, I shall not be moved, therefore my heart is glad and my glory rejoices, my flesh also shall rest in hope."

The major temple you must attend to is your life and your stand in God's presence.

It is unbelievable that the devil has caused major distractions in the church today. Many Churches open early and close late and still come for evening service or house fellowship but yet still conduct services every day of the week. These distractions have taken members away from having a private relationship with God. Members have prayed and received prophesies that their lives and home will improve, yet things have remained worse and with a catalogue of tensions.

The church should reduce their public participation and allow members to have an adequate period of Communion with God so that the miracles ministers of God have promised them to burst forth in their lives.

The devil is also persecuting the church on building projects. He sees that the church has considered building project as proof of christian success and has excessively occupied their minds with building church auditorium. People often discard old ones and begin anew. Some aspire to construct grand structures to be the largest and finest globally. Your heart follows where your treasure lies. Both the leaders and the members will have their minds concentrated on the building projects. Demolishing structures is something the devil often urges persecutors to do. If you want to finish a man touch his treasure house, you will see how empty he is. God is aware of the pulling down and vandalism of the structures. Why did God not avenge his elects? It is because as far as heaven is concerned, church building is not a major issue of eternal life. None of the stones in these buildings, no matter how high and impressive, will remain intact. The leading of the Holy Spirit is necessary for churches to embark on church building. It is crucial for leaders to understand that both heaven and earth, as well as all buildings, are being preserved for fire.

2 Peter 3:7-14
The same word for fiery judgement and perdition of the

ungodly men preserves the heavens and the earth, existing now.

But beloved, be not ignorant of this one thing, that one day is with the Lord as a thousand years and a thousand years as one day.

The Lord is not slack concerning his promise, as some men count slackness; but is long-suffering towards us, not willing that any should perish but that all should come to repentance. But the day of the Lord will come as a thief in the night; in which the heavens shall pass away with a great noise and the elements shall melt with fervent heat. Fire will destroy the earth and everything in it.

Considering that all these

things will eventually be dissolved, how should you behave in terms of holy conversation and godliness? Anticipating the day of God's coming, when the heavens will ignite and the elements will dissolve in scorching heat. However, we eagerly await a new heaven and a new earth as promised. Beloved, since you seek these things, be diligent to be found in peace, without blemish and blameless.

## GOSPEL AND POLITICS

Gospel and politics are two opposing camps, or Christianity and government have opposing ideologies. Politics is the art and science of directing the administration of government. And from experience, this is not totally correct. It is glaring from observation that those in power have very little time to administer the state. Their focus is on retaining power, which requires significant time and resources. Most of the state's funds were used to maintain political control, with only a small portion allocated to administration. Power acquisition is the key word in politics, corruption is the path, and wrestling is the game. The underlying concept of politics is that the system in operation is not good enough, therefore there is a need for change. The system is the focus, as opponents outside the corridor of power fight to introduce their supposedly better system, while the incumbent defends his own system's superiority.

The essence of Christianity is to expand missions. Their commitment lies in church planting to save the lost humanity. The Christian Church is resolute in accomplishing this singular mission through any necessary means.

Christianity is not concerned with the system of government, but man. To the Christians, there is nothing wrong with the system in operation but with the operators of the system. This opposing ideology has set the Christians in collision with government operators and has led to their constant persecution by operators of government in power. Jesus commanded the church to make disciples from every nation. This explicit command points to one truth that the condition of man is unacceptable to God, his creator, and for him to make a change by partaking in the divine nature of Christ.

Politics is saying system is the problem, get it changed but Christianity is saying man is the problem, get him transformed hence there is bound to be conflict. Politics, no matter how well branded, there will always be an element of corruption while Christianity is talking of truth and honesty. Christianity differs and distinct from politics and their weapon is not political power but spiritual. The power of God to salvation is for everyone who believes in Christ. Every Christian at an individual level shares this focus and channels his or her resources and efforts to the fact that they are called to save mankind and not to change the world. Tribulation is to be expected by Christians for their different ideologies, as nowhere did Jesus say they will escape tribulation and persecution. There is no amount of public relations that can change the world's disapproval to the Christians or the church.

Jesus said in John 15:20,

"Remember the word I said unto you, the servant is not greater than his Lord, if they persecute me they will persecute you also; if they have kept my sayings, they will keep yours as well."

The church entered the darkest period of its existence in the 4th century, which made it to lose its sense of focus because of passing through fire of persecution. The state killed many Christians, confiscated their church properties, burned some, and destroyed many others. However, because of their resilience, many pagans turned and became Christians. Emperor Constantine, the pagan ruler, brought about the change of focus by favoring the church. The state gave back all their properties and provided them with favors, clergymen received grants and tax exemption. The church's wealth in lands, houses, and properties made it beneficial to convert to Christianity. Many influential and wealthy individuals became Christians, leading to an inadvertent alliance between the church and state with significant influence.

Over time, church and state politics became entangled, causing confusion among church leaders. The church lost its purpose and remains in darkness till now. The present-day church is trending in the same way. Prominent church leaders are urging Christians to engage in state politics, posing a significant threat to the church and showing a lack of clarity and focus on the mission commanded by Jesus Christ.

One happy truth is that the church have very rich past to guide the present. It is ironic that very few Christians of this generation have little idea of what happened in the past and talk less about drawings lessons from it for guidance. The discipline of interpreting the past belongs to the realm of leadership that comfort, pleasure has overwhelmed, and too much freedom. This is a whirlwind that blows no good for the church. The foundation is gradually being destroyed and the righteous among them are prone to persecution and death

# CHAPTER FIVE
## THE LAST DAYS

ACTS 2:17-21 "And it shall come to pass in the last days, says the Lord. I will pour out my spirit on all people, and your sons and daughters will prophesy. Your young men shall see visions, and your old men shall dream dreams. In those days, I will pour out my spirit on my servants and handmaidens, and they will prophesy. I will display miraculous wonders in the sky and signs on the ground, including blood, fire, and smoke. Before the great and notable day of the Lord comes, the sun will turn into darkness and the moon into blood. And it shall come to pass: whoever calls on the name of the Lord will receive salvation.

From what we've observed, it's clear that the last movement of Christ is upon us and the events of the apocalypse, as described in Revelation 6, have started.

THE FIRST SEAL - GOSPEL.

According to Revelation 6:2, a rider on a white horse emerged with a bow, a crown, and a mission to conquer. This has to do with Christ coming in victory, power and the glory of his kingdom.

The rider is determined to

conquer, regardless of the world's disapproval. Christ will replace world governance with his own system. He will also replace the worship of deities or any other forms with the gospel worship of the kingdom of God on earth. The kingdom of God is universal-it includes all God's people of all dispensations, including the church. The kingdom of God and the kingdom of heaven are not two separate kingdoms, but they comprise the same kingdom. People from all races who believe in the gospel of Jesus Christ make up the church that is promised eternal life. The gospel will successfully reach all nations, ushering in a golden era of global submission to Christ. Jesus' return will bring an end to this present evil age, while the present manifestation continues alongside with it. The kingdom of heaven is the specific manifestation of the rule of God by Christ on earth over all nations, people, race and kindred. God's purpose reaches its peak in the church, fulfilling his central plan. There is a special favor shown to Christians as recipients of the covenant, but the blessings come through their being in Christ and not by some reversion to any type of relationship.

Jesus did not offer the Jews an earthly kingdom and himself their earthly king, as many people supposed. He came to bring a spiritual kingdom first and will set up his earthly kingdom when he returns.

The kingdom of God is a present reality. Christ is already ruling in the hearts of men and women.

Luke 17:20
The Pharisees asked Jesus when the kingdom of God would come, and he responded. The kingdom of God does not arrive with obvious signs, and people won't point and say "look here" or "look there," because it exists within you.

The laws of God, ingrained in an individual's heart, ensure the enduring truth of this statement.

The gospel will be preached

throughout the world as a testimony to all nations, as stated in Matthew 24:14.

Currently, missionaries have preached the gospel of Jesus Christ in every nation, but acceptance varies.

## THE SECOND SEAL - WAR.

In Revelation 6:3-4, when the Lamb opened the second seal, I heard the second living creature say, "Come!" and another horse, fiery red, emerged. Its rider was conferred with the ability to remove peace from the earth and cause men to kill one another. In addition, they gave him an enormous sword.

Let us not beat around the

bush. We have lost peace in the world. There is no part of the world you turn where there is no war. There are political crises, famine, economic problems, food crises, terrorism, killings and social disharmony in some areas. You have kingdoms fighting against kingdoms, but where you have relative calm, you cannot but hear the drums of the sound of war. There are indications of impending major wars ahead.

Jesus said such things must happen, but the end is not yet. The United Nations that is saddled with the responsibility of maintaining world peace is becoming incapable of doing so as the major super powers holding it together are gradually falling apart and the center cannot hold.

THE THIRD SEAL- FAMINE.

In Revelation 6:5, the third living creature proclaims the arrival of a black horse and its rider holding scales. I heard a voice among the four living creatures saying a quart of wheat costs a day's wages, and three quarts of barley also cost a day's wages, but don't harm the oil and wine.

This prophecy is for Russia and Ukraine, the two major world producers of barley and wheat. The voice warned them to refrain from war so that they do not damage their oil and wine. Obviously, the two nations will suffer untold hardship, economic woes, create famine, food crisis in the world, they will lose human and material resources, they will destabilize the peace and enjoyment of the world. They will cause a grave energy crisis and by tampering with their oil it will cause doom for them, also pains and hardship for the rest of the world.

## THE FOURTH SEAL - DEATH

Revelation 6:7-8. When the fourth seal was opened by the Lamb, I heard the voice of the fourth living creature saying, "Come." I looked and saw a pale horse with its rider called Death, followed closely by Hades. They were given power over a fourth of the earth to kill by sword, famine, plague and by wild beasts of the earth.

The prophesy of the fourth seal came to pass with the COVID-19 pandemic.

The pale horse suggests sickness. The plague shook the world to its core, causing medical services to be overwhelmed. Across the world, the killer horse (death) unexpectedly killed an unprecedented number of people. The World Health Organization (WHO) put the death rate at Seven Million People and many more are still dying. As many people were unprepared, Hades closely followed and prematurely dragged them into hell fire. The wild beasts referred to world leaders who are power drunks and who want to exert authority and dominion over other nations, people, races and kindred by declaring wars against one another, aggravating more premature deaths. These beasts inflicted pains, sufferings and untold hardship upon millions of people across the world. The aftermath of war created a food crisis, energy crisis, economic woes, political crisis and civil unrest around the world. There is no section of the world you turn into where there is no insecurity. Death had become a cankerworm, threatening the entire universe.

## THE FIFTH SEAL - THE GREAT TRIBULATION

Revelation 6:9
When he had opened the fifth

seal, I saw under the altar the souls of them that were slain for the word of God and for the testimony which they held; and they cried with a loud voice, saying, how long, O Lord, holy and true, will you not judge and avenge our blood on them that dwell on the earth? Until their fellow servants and brethren, who would be killed like them, were fulfilled, each of them received white robes to rest for a short time.

Unprecedented distress will occur, unlike anything ever witnessed before. The super powers will engage in a self-destructive war, shaking the world to its core. To save the chosen ones, Jesus will shorten the days, otherwise no one would survive.

The triumphant super power will subdue others, and they will be subject to him in control and service. The Leader of such power will be Anti-religion, he will ban all forms of worship. Religion will be forbidden and any gathering that has worship or religious inclination will attract the death penalty. Other religious sects will succumb to the Antichrist, but the Christians will not. They will raise high their voices of opposition; they will gather in secret places for worship. The government of Antichrist will face criticism from many leaders regarding its rule and activities. The leader's assassination is imminent, and a significant number of Christians will also lose their lives.

The government of Antichrist

will hunt and kill them in churches, in camps, and anywhere they gather. The intensity of the tribulation would be too great, and then Christ will reveal himself from heaven. Christ's glorious presence in the sky will be the sign that he is about to return to the earth. No disciple is to fear the appearance of Christ. His coming will be open and obvious to all. It will be like the lightning visible from the East to the West. A heart-shaped rainbow encircles his face, bold and visible. His eyes resemble marble stone. The saints behold it joyfully, while sinners and evildoers dread to gaze upon it. Sinners will find it uneasy to look at Christ in the sky because it will have a damaging effect on them. Unrighteousness can blind many, like staring at a high-intensity mid-day sun.

Many of the dead in Christ will resurrect and rapture, while many strange and fearful things will occur in the sky and on earth below. Believers of other faiths will convert to Christianity. It will be like a worldwide revival seeing the face of Christ in the air. It is enough proof that Jesus is the Messiah and the savior of the world. His visible presence is enough to convince the world that he is the true Messiah. Christ will reign in the heart of the people. The leaders, the rulers and the powers of the earth will be impotent and powerless. Their destructive weapons will be paralyzed and non -effective. His appearance alone will create fears in the heart of all sundry. The gods, deities, demons and other occult powers will be demobilized. They will flee and hide themselves inside rocks, mountains, and secret places to be obscured from the presence of Christ. This Christ differs from the gentle Jesus that came at the first coming. His first coming was to bring to mankind the accurate knowledge of the only true God, show the way of salvation and eternal life, but this time he came for judgement and it is a period of fear and panic. The Bible says, who can wait to behold his face? He whom the earth and the heavens fled before his presence, meaning the powers in heavenly places and the earth below, cannot withstand the pronouncement of his judgement. The powers of the world would be silent before him. There is nothing like super power, otherwise the angels will strike such power for destruction just like Sodom and Gomorrah. After the great tribulation comes the COSMIC CRISIS, which will be followed by the second coming of Christ.

## THE SIXTH SEAL: THE COSMIC CRISIS

Revelation 6:12-17

I watched as he opened the sixth seal. There was a great earthquake. The sun turned black like sackcloth made of goat's hair, the whole moon turned blood red and the stars of heaven fell to earth as late fig tree when shaken by a strong wind. Like a rolled-up scroll, the sky receded and made the mountains and islands disappear. The rulers, nobles, military leaders, wealthy individuals, and people from all works of life sought shelter in caves and among mountain rocks. They cried out to the mountains and rocks, pleading for them to fall on us and shield us from the one on the throne and the Lamb's anger." For the great day of their wrath has come, and who can stand?

There is no reason for the righteous to panic, but the evil-doers are in great jeopardy, their existence is from minute to minute as destruction can catch up with them unawares. When Jesus appeared in the sky, he reduced the brightness of the sun to the barest minimum, the residue which is red reflected on the moon and sends red light to the earth. That alone created the first panic on the earth. Jesus shook the powers of the sky. The presence of Christ caused Satan, the devil who is Lucifer, and Dragon, Apollon, and the realm of darkness to scatter in fear. Many of the heavenly powers fell down from the sky and died like men.

According to Psalm 82:5-7, those who walk in darkness cause the earth's foundations to be disrupted. God called them gods and children of the most high, yet they will perish like mortals and descend like princes.

The commotion caused by the appearance of Christ makes the sky to skip and roll and destabilize the powers of the sky and that of the earth, rocks, trees, mountains were transposed from their position. The mischief makers, the unbelievers, the wicked leaders and those who do abominable things will hide their faces from Christ because the hour of judgement has come and who can wait?

All the nations of the earth will mourn, they will see the Son of Man coming on the clouds of the sky with power and great glory. Christ will reign over the earth from heaven and the gospel will successfully reach all nations. No one will need to preach the gospel, since Christ's presence in the cloud will make him known to everyone. Mysterious phenomena will unfold in both the sky and on earth.

Countless miracles, signs, and wonders will occur, leaving everyone astonished.

Jesus goes to speak about the rapture Matthew 24:31.

And he will send his angels with a loud trumpet call and they will gather his elect from the four winds, from one end of the heavens to the other.

The removal of the saints and the church is essential for the impending wrath of God on the earth, which occurs after the Seventh seal is opened (Revelation 8 and 9).

THE MEETING IN THE AIR

Believers will meet the Lord in the air. At the end of the

tribulation, they will accompany him to the earth.

The remaining living saints will be caught up together with them in the clouds. The seventh seal's opening will bring God's wrath upon the earth and the evil ones, and He will rapture His children.

## THE SEVENTH SEAL: THE WRATH OF GOD POURED OUT ON THE EARTH

Upon opening the seventh seal, an angel received a substantial amount of incense to offer with the prayers of the saints. The smoke of the incense, blended with the prayers, rose before God.

Seven angels were prepared to punish the earth for the death of the saints.

Revelation 8:7-12

Following the first angel's trumpet, a mixture of hail, fire, and blood fell, scorching a third of the trees and all the green grass on the earth.

The second angel sounded his trumpet and cast a great mountain burning with fire into the sea. This caused a third of the sea to turn into blood, and a third of the creatures in the sea, as well as those with life, died. In addition, a third of the ships were lost.

The third angel blew his trumpet, causing a bright star to fall from the sky. It landed on a third of the rivers and fountains, turning the water bitter. Many people died.

The fourth angel struck one-third of the sun, moon, and stars, causing them to darken and not shine for one-third of the day.

An angel flying through the midst of the air was saying with a loud voice, woe, woe, woe to the inhabitants of the earth by the plagues which are yet to come.

Revelation 9:1-4

The fifth angel sounded his trumpet, and I saw a star that had fallen from the sky to the earth. The star received the key to the Abyss's shaft. When he opened the Abyss, smoke rose from it like the smoke from a gigantic furnace. The smoke from the Abyss darkened the sun and sky. Locusts descended from the smoke, possessing earth-like scorpion powers. They were told not to harm the grass of the earth or any plant or tree, but only those people who did not have the seal of God on their foreheads.

They were told not to kill them, but to torment them for five months, like a scorpion's sting. And in those days shall men seek death and shall not find it, and shall desire to die and death shall flee from them.

The sixth angel loose the four angels which are bound on River Euphrates having riders with breast plate of fire, fire killed the third part of men and by smoke and by brimstone which issued out of their mouths.

And the rest of the people which were not killed repented not of their evil deeds, neither repented they of their sorceries nor of their fornication, they repented not of the works of their hands that they should not worship devils and idols of gold and silver, brass and stone and of wood.

However, the wrath of God subdued the Antichrist and the evil ones, and there was a long period of peace prior to the millennium.

# CHAPTER SIX
## THE MILLENNIUM

THE MILLENNIUM is the one thousand years of a peaceful rule of Christ over the earth which is spoken of in Revelation 20:4 "I saw the souls of them that were beheaded for the witness of Jesus Christ and for the word of God and which had not worshiped the beast neither his image neither had received his mark upon their foreheads or in their hands and they lived and reigned with Christ a thousand years."

This is the primary reference in the Bible that specifically mentioned One Thousand years of Messiah rule over all the earth.

By the manifestation of Christ in the sky every nation will embrace the gospel of Jesus Christ resulting in the resurrection of the dead across the globe Rapture will occur in churches, gatherings, along the streets, at Mills, on the farms, places of work, anywhere and everywhere. Thereafter, Christ will return with the raptured saints for the millennium.

There will be a long period of peace over the earth called the millennium. Choice of religion is eliminated but only that of Jesus Christ. God will showcase the victory of Christ's kingdom and glorify his name over all the earth.

At the end of the millennium, Christ will withdraw for the devil to tempt them in order to know who among them is worthy of eternal life.

Subsequently, Christ will return once more in his physical body to conclude this era and begin the eternal age.

However, it is worthy of note that one thousand years spoken of in Revelation 20:4 is the only literal reference in the Bible to a specifically One Thousand years rule of Christ. Other references in the Bible speak of golden age, hence one thousand years may be symbolic.

At the end of the millenium, there will come a time of apostasy and the reign of Antichrist. The devil will test and tempt those who passed through the millennium.

The initial resurrection is the physical resurrection of the righteous, occurring when Christ returns during the millennium. However, when Christ returns to conclude the world, the physical resurrection of both the righteous and the unrighteous will occur. After this comes the white throne judgement of eternal ages and the last state of all mankind.

# CHAPTER SEVEN
## THE FINAL END

WHEN THE millennium is over, Satan shall be let loose out of his prison and he will go out to deceive the nations which are in the four corners of the world. He will gather Gog and Magog to wage war against the saints of God. Satan will deceive the people who passed through the millennium. He will perform many deceptive miracles, signs, and wonders. He will oppose Christ, exalt himself above God, and show himself to be God and will raise himself above all that is

87

called God in the temple and say that he himself is God, demanding worship. Many people will believe him and he will lead them to be lost forever. They will join his army to wage war on the saints of God. Their numbers will be as vast as the sand of the seashore, encircling the camp of the saints throughout the earth. In battle, the Gog and Magog will team up against the children of God. The weapon of the children of God are not carnal but spiritual and mighty. The children of God will call upon God and He will send down fire from heaven to consume them, and then they will be cast into the lake of fire.

The White Throne Judgement.

Revelation 20:12 describes how the dead, both small and great, stood before God. God opened the books, including the book of Life, and judged the dead based on their works as recorded in the books.

Death and Hell were cast into the lake of fire and anyone whose name was not written in the book of life was cast into the lake of fire. This is the second death.

The new heaven and the new earth will merge, the Tabernacle of God will be with men. God will wipe away all tears from their eyes. Death, sorrow, crying, and pain shall be no more, as the past has faded away.

According to Revelation 21:22, there is no temple in the place described as the Lord God Almighty and the Lamb serve as the temple.

The city didn't require the sun or moon to illuminate it, as the glory of God illuminated it and the

Lamb is its light. The saints shall see the face of God and his name shall be on their foreheads.

And the end will come when Jesus will hand over the kingdom to God the Father after he has destroyed all dominion, authority and Power. When he had done this, Jesus will subject himself to God his Father so that God will be all in all.

# ABOUT THE AUTHOR

Pastor Emmanuel Olufemi Ayekoloye is the Vicar-in charge of Lord of Restoration Family Worship Ministry. He is a Herald of God who carries messages of divine impact to reform this generation and one of the end-time Voices of God. He is an Alumnus of the University of Ife Ile-Ife, Nigeria; International University, Missouri, USA and World Pastors College, Akure, Nigeria. Married to co-planter of the ministry, Evangelist (Mrs.) Christianah Kikelomo Ayekoloye and blessed with children.

Pastor Emmanuel loves to hear from his reader. You can send your message to eayekoloye@gmail.com.